# DEAR HAPPY GHOSTS

# DEAR HAPPY GHOSTS

*Scenes from the Outram Picture Archive*

$$\frac{1898}{1990}$$

*Commentary by*
## William Hunter
*Introduction by*
## Arnold Kemp

MAINSTREAM
PUBLISHING

IN CONJUNCTION WITH

Glasgow Herald

EVENING Times

Copyright © George Outram & Co, 1990
All rights reserved
Published in Great Britain in 1990 by
MAINSTREAM PUBLISHING COMPANY
(EDINBURGH) LTD
7 Albany Street
Edinburgh EH1 3UG
ISBN 1 85158 371 8 (cloth)

British Cataloguing in Publication Data
Kemp, Arnold
Dear happy ghosts: Scenes from the Outram Picture
Archive 1898-1990.
1. Scotland. Strathclyde Region. Glasgow. Social
life, 1901
I. Title    II. Hunter, William
941.443082

ISBN 1-85158-371-8

Design and Finished Artwork by James Hutcheson and Paul Keir

Typeset in 10/12 Sabon by Novatext Graphix Limited, Edinburgh
Printed in Great Britain by Butler and Tanner Ltd, Frome

# Contents

INTRODUCTION
7

CROWDED CITY
11

LIVING IT UP
77

RIVERSIDE SHUFFLE
91

BRIGHT LIGHTS
111

RED TO ORANGE
127

AT WAR
167

SOME REVOLTING GENTLEMEN
175

COFFEE STOP
181

PHOTO FINISH
189

APPENDIX
191

*To Outram photographers past and present*

Taken directly from the Outram Picture Library, it is interesting to note
that the photographs in this volume show evidence of the original printer's
cropping and retouching.

ARNOLD KEMP

# Introduction

THE TITLE OF THIS COLLECTION OF PICTURES IS AN ALLUSION TO A FINE POEM called 'You lived in Glasgow' written by Iain Crichton Smith in 1972*. The poet discloses that he left Glasgow, his birthplace, at the age of two. He sits in George Square 'under a 1970 sky':

> You were happier here than anywhere, you said.
> Such fine good neighbours helping when your child
> almost died of croup. Those pleasant Wildes
> removed with the fallen rubble have now gone
> in the building programme which renews each stone.
> I stand in a cleaner city, better fed,
> in my diced coat, brown hat, my paler hands
> leafing a copy of the latest book.
> Dear ghosts, I love you, haunting sunlit winds,
> dear happy dented ghosts, dear prodigal folk.

The changes that have overtaken Glasgow even in the last decade are evident to those who have no older memories and startling to those who return after a long absence. Charing Cross, Cowcaddens and Townhead are still names on the map and the road-signs; but the old tenement communities have largely gone. Gorbals no longer even has an official existence, the name expunged by town planners along with the tenements (replaced by much reviled high flats). The trams which give so strong a signature to many street scenes down the years have been retired, though there is now talk of bringing them back. The horse-and-cart is occasionally seen being driven by a descendant of the rag-and-bone men and carters who once were everywhere.

The picture archive of George Outram & Co is not the only source of evidence of the way things were in Glasgow. There are other fine collections. But the eye of the press photographer is not that of the recording angel. He (or she) is not systematic but follows the news — is driven where the wind blows. What is news today is not news tomorrow, and the events which stirred distant times may seem odd and even trivial now. But, in the process of pursuing the news, the press photographer adds, whether intentionally or not, to the accumulations of social history.

For my money the pictures gathered here are about people power. Nothing is more interesting to men or women than another human being. I have often noticed at concerts, or in the theatre, even at the most absorbing event, how a late-comer or an early-leaver will distract attention from the stage and become a cynosure. The faces which shine out of these old pictures do seem like happy ghosts. It is their almost universal cheerfulness which speaks down the years. Even soldiers about to go off to war communicate a certain gaiety of spirit. Wartime evacuees clearly enjoy the break from routine. Sometimes, it is true, we note puzzlement and a wariness of the camera, but what mostly shines out of these pictures is an innocence derived from pleasures that might today be regarded as unsophisticated. The happiness of the dancers at the Dennistoun Palais as they line up at the (unlicensed) coffee bar is most engaging.

There is also, in many shots, a greater sense of public decorum than we would expect today. The lord provosts who make occasional appearances in these pictures are people of dignity and their processions are solemn affairs, reflecting the importance of the city. The Royal Family and civic leaders are much more informal today, perhaps because we live in an age in which TV has made the public intimate with those who lead them. A price has been paid, perhaps, in lost respect or the degeneration of the Royal Family's life into a kind of peep-show.

Even the strikers and the agitators seem a respectable lot. Glasgow saw a great deal of political turbulence and unrest during the First World War but those who organised the resistance to high rents and appalling housing look impressive down the years; even John Maclean, that thorn in the flesh of governments, in and out of jail with some regularity during and after the war, looks a gentle and jolly soul. The Glasgow poet Edwin Morgan* wrote:

> Maclean was not naïve, but
> 　　　　　　　　'We are out
> for life and all that life can give us'
> was what he said, that's what he said.

When we came to choose these pictures, we relied heavily on the personal knowledge of the archive of our picture librarians, particularly Bill Doig and Robert Tweedie. There are about 5½ million prints on file. I cannot believe that Bill and Robert have instant recall of every single one, but there were times when I wondered, so impressive was their ability quickly to retrieve pictures vaguely remembered by others. We were eclectic in our approach: we made no attempt to produce a systematic pictorial history, because there are, in the file, periods both of glut and famine. A comprehensive pictorial history of Glasgow would have to draw on other collections also. Rather we chose pictures which retained interest either because of their human content or because they communicated the atmosphere of their times. Certain themes, however, began to emerge — war, politics, occasions, vanished townscapes, people at work and play, and so on. A picture editor, rebuking a reporter, is once supposed to have said: 'A picture is worth 1,000 words — and in your case 2,000 words.' However, words and pictures are both at their best when they reinforce each other. The task of writing the text to accompany the pictures was undertaken by William Hunter, a member of the *Glasgow Herald* staff for more than 20 years. His weekly column gives me and thousands of our readers much pleasure. He has, I think, enjoyed his walk among the clear-eyed and smiling ghosts, his only regret being that his beloved Paisley does not even have a walk-on part, though, before even having read the text, I was utterly confident that he would find some way of mentioning that celebrated burgh. His final manuscript confounded me in that respect but delighted me in others. He has taken this collection of photographs as a starting point for a series of poignant evocations of the great city which it celebrates.

Finally it should be remembered that these pictures come not only from the pages of the *Herald* and *Evening Times* but also from the *Bulletin*, published from 1915 to 1960. Older Glaswegians still lament its passing. It was a picture paper and its legacy to us a greatly enriched archive.

*Published in *Noise and Smokey Breath: An Illustrated Anthology of Glasgow Poems 1900-1983* (Third Eye Centre and Glasgow District Libraries Publications Board)

WILLIAM HUNTER

# Crowded City

Keelie: a male city-dweller of the rougher sort, specifically of Glasgow and district, occasionally of Edinburgh; an uncouth rowdy fellow, a tough.
*Scottish National Dictionary*

PEOPLE APPEARED IN THE FIRST DOCUMENTARY PICTURES OF THE AULD TOON by accident. They happened to be there, idling around their front doors. From the photographer there was no request for a smile. Blank and bemused stares satisfied him. People weren't part of his assignment. He saw them as extras. The first keelies to be in photos were treated as bystanders of their own lives. Not them, but the streets where they lived were the subject.

Like much of the work in this book, the scenes which Thomas Annan photographed in the pends and wynds off High Street and the Saltmarket are treasured for negative reasons. They have become not what the cameraman saw. Time has added the value of aspects which escaped the eye. Annan thought he was taking views of architecture. Passing years developed his series of 31 photos into a bleakly sensitive record of poor lives. Commissioned by the town council to compose a file of some interesting landmarks about to be demolished, he created a haunting documentary that was the world's first unblinking look at people in slums. In 1868 it was just another assignment that made Annan the city's first photo-journalist. While he didn't mind when out of numb curiosity some of the inhabitants strayed into his lens, he didn't ask them to be in the picture.

His task was to photograph heritage. With a renewed Trongate for its core, an industrial way of city living was being invented that had not been attempted anywhere in the world. Then, as now, economic change had obliged the keelies to start a new day. They could not be sure where they were going. With images from a past that was being obliterated, the city's leaders wanted souvenirs of where they had been. They were seeking firm ground in which to embed the next chapter of the story. Before Glasgow could flourish again, they thought it had better know its roots.

Newspaper photographers, Annan's children, continue his work without having time often to think about that side of their trade. Theirs is a quick, nervy business. Their snaps (as they call them) are not taken for posterity. Pictures have a life of one day. That's with luck, and if editors smile upon them. Most snaps never see newsprint. They accumulate in brown library envelopes of rejection. If they may fade there, they don't die. Although more perishable than peaches, news snaps can last forever. If age withers them, it can enliven them. Some photos mature and some change. Solemn scenes of pomp and importance start to look ridiculous;

plain, quiet, little family-album snaps acquire significance, even magic. Some photos in this picture-book give the old place back its youth. Strong faces don't age in them.

Formal history sees in these prints years of city decline that came within a few stumbles of a fall. Glasgow has been fading for all of this century. Moments have been captured which give glimpses and personal reminders of when it seemed to have come nigh to its end. Sometimes the very houses seem asleep. But unless the pictures are fibbing it has been a great way to go. Here is a city that, half-alive, has kept kicking. With some snaps it helps to take Annan's way of ignoring who the people are to concentrate on where they are. In the manner that pantomime audiences at the old Alhambra Theatre and the older Metropole used to applaud the scenery, the main act of a cityscape can be a building. If a monument is needed to salute just one spectacular achievement that is not a legacy of a Victorian high noon, look at Hampden Park. Never mind the crowd at a big game, get a load of the park! It embodies a spirit of romantic hard-headedness and practical dreaming that urban decline is supposed to be unable to contain. Yet Hampden *is*. So familiar a geographical feature has it grown to be that it is treated as a natural phenomenon. It is seen as eternal as a mountain. Even its name is assumed to be God-given. Why Hampden? The answer that comes is that Hampden is, well, Hampden. Keelies forget that it took three men of vision to make it happen; and they were toffs in bowler hats at that who got the job done. They were even, heaven forfend, a committee.

Because of their love for the amateur game, Queen's Park Football Club had already surrendered the high ground of champions to the ascent of paid gladiators when they decided to create the greatest stadium in the world. With eerie optimism, a dozen acres of farmland were acquired for twice as many readies as there were in the bank. Perhaps the men with the educated feet saw it as a shrine to their own glorious beginnings. It was to be their third Hampden. All of them were called after a row of neighbouring houses which had taken its name from an English rebel Member of Parliament. Names which matter more, and ought to be roared like a half-back line of renown, were Geake, Lawrence and Sellar. Forgotten men, they were the part-time entrepreneurs who decreed the stately pleasuredome. It held its first match (Queen's won) in October 1903.

Uncle Arthur Geake, an adopted keelie born in Nottingham, was a grain merchant, otherwise Mr Hampden. Five times he was club president. Despite the adventurous wisdom of his leadership — the debts on the big bowl were paid off in seven years — he stayed homely and avuncular. According to Queen's Park legend, he upbraided a player who pulled a weed from the pitch. It was Uncle Arthur's conviction that he had the secret of keeping the turf sweet so that a pulled weed would never grow again. For keeping to simple straightforward ways in the grandest of circumstances, A. Geake had learned a keelie trick. An enduring gift of the citizenry is to remain themselves, wherever. Public occasions of great pomp can be turned by them into a street party. Elaborate festivities become local fêtes. When formal behaviour elsewhere would be *de rigueur*, the keelies become villagers again. Even at their historic encounter in 1967 in George Square with Alexei Nikolayevich Kosygin, Chairman of the Council of Ministers of the USSR, no less, their mateyness ruled.

Although every picture tells a story, the snap of Mr Kosygin in the square cannot have the full tale. Despite an off-stage orchestration of riflemen strung along surrounding roofs, what threatened to be a stiff visitation was transformed into hearty vaudeville, scripted by patter merchants. Played as per programme, the meeting promised the punters no chance for a carry-on. There were polis everywhere. At the start of the show Mr Kosygin wore his sad clown's face. He was the sort of chum whose idea of spending a Saturday morning was to inspect a power station. Besides, he was from farther away in the cold East than even Edinburgh. None of it was promising material at all.

After Hunterston, he attended a tousy game of football at Kilmarnock where Rangers were visiting. Rugby Park was packed. 'Kosygin,' the hordes cried, 'cha cha cha.' They sang to him: 'We'll keep the blue flag flying high.' Mr Kosygin beamed, he waved. He was ready for them because he had been well rehearsed earlier in the square. He had got the message. Even the CND banners had made a joke. 'Welcome to your No 1 target, Mr Kosygin,' they proclaimed. Four thousand smiles said a simpler hello. His fierce blue eyes brightened. He began to look enchanted. If there was a problem, it was up to those damned photographers. They took a million historic snaps and most of the room. So thick a swarm of them surrounded their target, they threatened to spoil the event they were supposed to be recording for evermore. Amen to that, the crowd complained, not quietly. They shouted that they couldn't see the rabbit. A uniformed constable had enough of their moaning. He faced them: 'Would you like me to carry him over and show him to you?' So it was a laugh, what the hell? Nae problem. And then the kissing started.

Alexei spotted Craig Mabon, aged four months, and stopped to plant a cheeper on his white woolly hat. It gave his mother a chance to present the bunch of snowdrops she had brought specially. Inside the City Chambers Christine Moffat, the students' charities queen, waited to collect a fiver from Russia with love. He kissed her. Later at nuclear Hunterston, Margaret McKerrell, a canteen worker and mother of six, kissed him. Mrs McKerrell said she had just looked up and asked if she could give him a kiss: 'It was just a friendly gesture to make sure they'd see that there will be no more wars for my kids coming up.' Although nobody knew the word for it, in George Square had been discovered glasnost.

The precursor of the
Coca Cola ride at the
Garden Festival in 1988
was the water-chute at
the 1901 Glasgow
International
Exhibition. Here it has
deposited a boatload
into the lake. Behind
are the university and
the pavilion.

*Hampden was the scene of a serious riot in 1909 after the Celtic-Rangers match had ended in a draw. The crowd had hoped for extra time and, when denied, set fire to pay boxes and anything else that would burn. About 130 people were injured and the cup was withheld after two games ended drawn (2-2, 1-1). Hampden was closed for the rest of the season.*

*Migration is part of Glasgow's story. This delightful picture is of a family emigrating from Dumbarton to Canada in 1924.*

*Hampden Park around
1926.*

*Buchanan Street from
Argyle Street, undated.*

*The interior of the new premises of the Union Bank, Glasgow, 1927. The print is marked on the back: 'Sir Robert Bruce, [the Editor] would like this used in the page.' The Union Bank merged with the Bank of Scotland in 1955.*

*Crowds celebrate the opening of King George V Bridge, built to relieve severe congestion. King George V, with Queen Mary, laid its foundation stone in 1927. It was regarded as the most important structure in reinforced concrete in Britain at that time. It was opened the following February by the Lord Provost, Sir David Mason, who held office from 1926 to 1929.*

*The 'Umbrella',*
*Bridgeton Cross,*
*undated.*

*Gorbals Cross,
undated.*

*The corner of
Buchanan Street and
Argyle Street, 1928.*

*Bow's Jubilee Sail, 1933. A happy departure from the Broomielaw.*

*A publicity shot from 1929 of Sir Harry Lauder (left) with Doodles, a famous clown at the old Hengler's Circus.*

*John Thomson, the Celtic goalkeeper, was killed making a diving save at the feet of Sam English, in the Old Firm game of September 1931. This picture shows him, shortly before the tragic accident, in the prime of his athleticism, making a fine clearance from an Alan Morton cross.*

*The legendary Rangers winger, Alan Morton.*

*Charlie Shaw, he never saw*
*Where Alan Morton pit the ba'*
*He pit the ba' right in the net*
*And Charlie Shaw sat doon and gret.*

*Jimmy McGrory of Celtic playing against Motherwell in 1933.*

*Despite the blurring in the foreground, this picture gives a good general impression of the scene at Hampden in April 1935. This was probably the cup final between Rangers and Hamilton, which resulted in a 2-1 win for Rangers.*

*The widening of Great
Western Road at
Anniesland, 1936.*

*A Royal visit to
Bridgeton, 1933. The
pleasure given to
ordinary folk by such
occasions could not be
clearer. Two points
about the policemen —
their relative height and
their serene dignity.*

*Students' charities days,*
*then as now, raised*
*laughs as well as cash.*
*This ragged pipe band*
*paraded down*
*Sauchiehall Street in*
*1933.*

*Civic dignity is
personified by Lord
Provost Sir Patrick
Dollan as he addresses
pupils of St Anthony's
School, Govan,
probably in 1938, but
the camera is a
distraction to his
audience.*

*Address of loyalty at
the Trades House,
1935.*

*Hampden in May 1937.
For the cup final
between Aberdeen and
Celtic (which Celtic
won 2-1), there was the
highest attendance —
of 146,433 — ever
recorded in any club
match in Europe.*

*Sir William Burrell, who made his fortune in shipping, became the benefactor whose bequest eventually produced the Burrell Collection, which houses his eclectic collection. He is seen here in 1944, on horseback, on the Glorious Twelfth in the Lammermuirs. A guest, Lord Digby, is on the right.*

*Before the Clean Air Act: Union Street shortly after 10 a.m. on 26 November, 1936.*

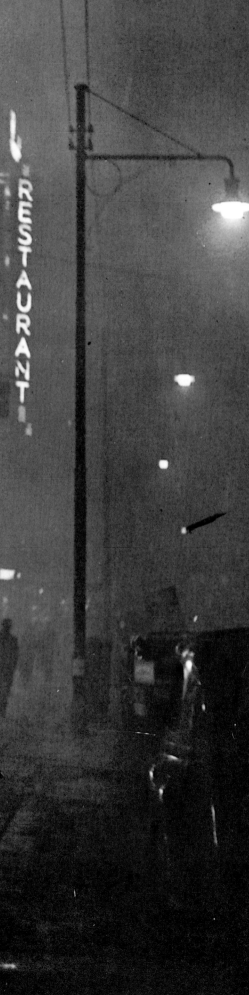

EX.1612.

We may deduce from the coats and hats that the sunshine was chilly at the Empire Exhibition of 1938. If so, it is an appropriate metaphor, for the sun was setting on the British Empire. The Second World War, which destroyed Britain's imperial power and exhausted its wealth, was a year away. A tower was a motif also of the Garden Festival 50 years later.

*In 1938, at the opening of the Empire Exhibition, there were no televised relays or hearing aids. The opening ceremony is described by a well-meaning commentator to a deaf, dumb and blind group.*

*Crowds await the royal opening of the Empire Exhibition in 1938. Here is the atmosphere of a royal occasion before the age of television. You had to turn up to see it, but then you became part of it: you were more than a spectator. The smiles of the crowd, the flags and bunting, the almost palpable sense of anticipation — all suggest a quite genuine happiness in being part of a great day.*

*Dr O. H. Mavor (James Bridie), playwright and, in 1943, founder of the Citizens' Theatre, undated.*

Under the chairmanship of Dr Mavor (James Bridie) the Citizens' produced some outstanding talent, including Duncan Macrae and Stanley Baxter. Macrae was an incomparable actor and is seen here with James Gibson, a veteran of the pre-war Scottish National Players, in Bridie's Forrigan Reel, 1944.

Will Fyffe (left) is immortalised in his song 'I belong to Glasgow'. He is seen here in 1946 with Harry Gordon in Babes in the Wood at the Alhambra.

*High spirits in the open-air baths at Greenhead, 1947. The costas were in the future.*

*Beauty contests became big business after the war until they were discredited by the women's movement. There is a certain innocence about these beauty queens at a garden fête in the Pollok Estate, 1948.*

An open-air play by
Community House
Mobile Theatre at Keith
Street, Partick, 1950.
The play dealt with the
United Nations theme
on Lord Boyd Orr's
'Food for the World'
and was in aid of UNO.
The urchins on the
midden are up to no
good.

A Glasgow procession.
The Order of St John of
Jerusalem process from
the Cathedral to
Provand's Lordship,
1950.

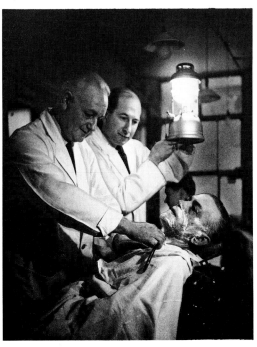

*The opening of the new
Hampden press box,
1952.*

*Glasgow in the dark: a
shave by storm lantern
for customers in
Dalmarnock, 1954. The
local power station had
been knocked out by an
explosion.*

*Universal cheeriness
and not a strong drink
in sight. The café at
Dennistoun Palais,
1957.*

*The decorum of the
Dennistoun Palais as
dancers leave, 1957.*

*Dance No 23, a quickstep, at the Albert Ballroom, 1957. The watching ladies take tea.*

*Beside a Glasgow dance hall a taxi driver awaits his fare, 1957.*

*The neighbourliness of tenement life is fondly remembered. Jim Murphy, 74, is welcomed back to his single-end after a spell in hospital. He arrived home to find his neighbours and friends had installed a new fireplace, 1959.*

The office of Rector at Scottish universities traditionally produced robust and sometimes violent election campaigns. The installation of Mr R. A. (later Lord) Butler in 1958 saw such tumult reach a point beyond all reason. In disgraceful scenes the platform party was showered with flour and other missiles. Herald *photographer John Mackay (now chief photographer) was knocked unconscious by a flying cabbage. Apologies all round and disciplinary action ensued, and rectorials were never quite the same thereafter. What now seems remarkable about these pictures is the grave dignity maintained throughout by those who were the target of student exuberance. Lord Boyd Orr, pictured with a faintly smiling Rab Butler, kept his cool; but a certain gravity in his expression speaks of punishments to come.*

Herald *photographer*
*Mackay knocked*
*unconscious.*

*One of the great Hampden occasions was the European Cup final between Real Madrid and Eintracht Frankfurt in 1960. In a dazzling exhibition of attacking football, Real won 7-3. Here the great Di Stefano scores Real's final goal. Both teams were fêted by the crowd of 134,000.*

*Glasgow's now vigorous musical life owes a considerable debt to Sir Alexander Gibson, seen here with Yehudi Menuhin in 1962. Apart from his long association with the SNO as its principal conductor, he was founding father and musical director of Scottish Opera until 1987.*

*The Glasgow Empire was a graveyard of English comics. Ken Dodd said in 1965 in a TV interview: 'The trouble with Freud is that he never played the Glasgow Empire Saturday night.' It was closed in March 1963 when artists and staff joined the audience in 'Auld Lang Syne'.*

The importance of the Glasgow Stock Exchange, like that of others outside London, has been reduced by modern technology, but in 1959 it was still a busy floor. A young clerk marks up the prices, 1964.

*In the sixties popular culture was turned on its head, and the leading revolutionaries were the Beatles. They are seen with show compère Bob Bain at the Odeon Cinema in 1964.*

*A Methodist outing,*
*1965.*

*Hugh (later Lord) Fraser was one of Scotland's most remarkable businessmen. The culmination of his career was his acquisition of Harrods in 1959. He also successfully fought off Roy Thomson's bid for the Herald in 1964. He is seen here with the House of Fraser board in 1965. His arm is round the shoulder of his son and heir. It is very much a case of king, crown prince and courtiers. The directors (left to right) are E. Gamble, A. H. Gardiner, Hugh Fraser, Lord Fraser, A. Spence, I. A. Moffat and W. McLean. He died in 1966 and his son, Sir Hugh, died in 1987.*

*It is generally accepted that many of the tactics employed by Hugh Fraser in his many takeover battles would not be allowed today. Here he is seen giving a press conference in 1956.*

*Lord Fraser with
catering controller A. T.
Cameron at the opening
of Muirhead's
restaurant, 1956.*

*A happy picture of the late Rev. Dr Neville Davidson and his wife, with a lawnmower. It was one of the gifts presented to them on their retirement by the congregation of Glasgow Cathedral, 1967.*

*Alexei Kosygin, then the Soviet leader, received a warm welcome when he visited Glasgow in 1967. He is seen in George Square accompanied by John Johnston, Lord Provost from 1965 to 1969.*

*The Havergal régime at the Citizens' began controversially. The lieges were outraged by innovative productions of* Hamlet *and other plays. But it is now acknowledged that Giles Havergal, seen here outside the theatre in 1982, has, with his associates, built an international reputation for the company and extended its reach into the community. He was appointed Artistic Director in 1969.*

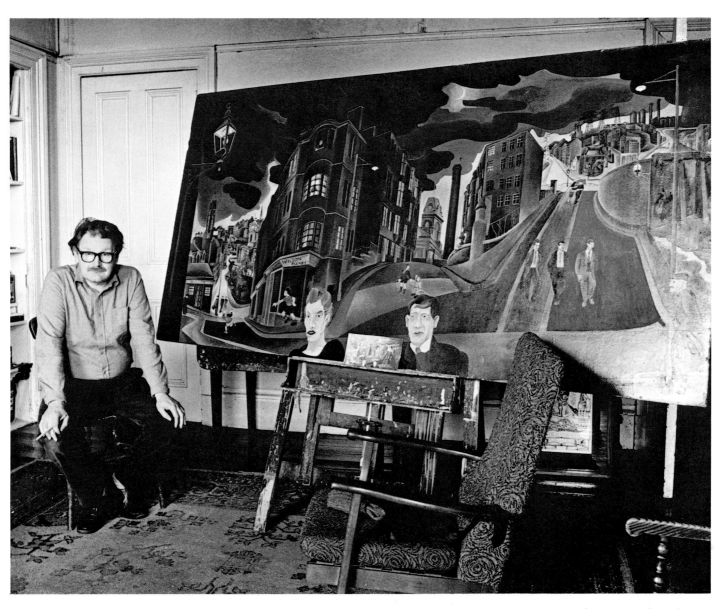

*The artist, novelist and poet, Alasdair Gray, with his painting* Cowcaddens in the Fifties.

*The visit of Pope John Paul II to Scotland in 1982 drew an enormous congregation to Bellahouston Park. The happiness of the occasion is well expressed by the cheerfulness of two priests warm in body and soul; and by the nun charmingly breaking the rhythm of grave meditation at the service in St Mary's Cathedral, Edinburgh.*

The Glasgow Marathon
was an important
milestone in the city's
revival in the eighties.
However, it did not
survive. The marathon
craze ebbed: many
amateur runners found
the distance too great.
The organisers of what
was a 'people's
marathon' were
unwilling to turn it into
a highly remunerated
professional event. We
see the runners going up
High Street in 1983.

*Arts graduands relax at*
*Wellington Church on*
*their big day in 1984.*

*Lady bowlers attend a service in Glasgow Cathedral, 1986.*

*The Horse Shoe is one of Glasgow's most famous bars. It still serves splendid traditional grub.*

*George Wyllie's work of art, Finnieston Crane, was one of the most striking images of Mayfest 1987. Its provenance can be easily seen from the accompanying picture of a steam loco, built by the North British Locomotive Company of Springburn, being loaded aboard an Ellerman liner for shipment to Bombay in 1933.*

*Glasgow's large Pakistani community turned out in force in 1987 to welcome Prime Minister Mohammed Khan Junejo. Here he listens to Hafiz Jamil Moghul, then aged eight, who has memorised the Koran.*

*The popular success of the Garden Festival in 1988 owed much to its funfair elements. For many Glaswegians their chief memory was of the Coca Cola ride. Apart from the thrill of defying gravity with its help, it became for a season a prominent part of the Glasgow skyline and its departure was regretted.*

*Open-air concert,*
*Gorbals, 1959.*

*Cars on the road, far less on the stage, were a novelty in 1921. This publicity shot shows a Wolsely car being used in the current production at the King's Theatre — a play called* Out to Win. *This work has now disappeared into obscurity but one suspects it contained the line: 'Anyone for tennis?'*

# Living it up

Oh ye cannae fling pieces oot a twenty storey flat,
Seven hundred hungry weans'll testify to that.
If it's butter, cheese or jeely, if the breid is plain or pan,
The odds against it reaching earth are ninety-nine tae wan.
Chorus of 'The Jeely Piece Song', by ADAM McNAUGHTAN

TENEMENTS ARE TRICKY TO DEFINE. HEIGHT, HOWEVER, HAS TO BE A PART OF the specification. They are flatted blocks of houses of the kind now called low-rise. Closes, or common entries, have also been lassoed into planners' lingo. They get designated as storey-high, slot-like orifices, although not in Maryhill. Most tenements have four storeys. They go up as many stairs as a reasonably fit and sensible person wants to climb home. Historically, tenements did not leave the ground so far that a coalman couldn't carry a 1 cwt bag up or a mother could throw a jeely piece down. Socially, the living has gone down as well as up. When Frank Worsdall, scholar of the Victorian city, in 1979 published his architectural study of keelie housing, entitled *The Tenement*, he wrote this bulldozer of a sentence: 'Tenements these days is a dirty word and is used almost exclusively to describe a slum property.'

Times and tenements change. How some masterpieces of last century have been scrubbed back to their red or 'white', meaning honey-coloured, stone has been the most startling single revelation of renewed streets. Now in the Merchant City middle-class pioneers pay suburban-semi prices to live on top of each other in converted warehouses and former sweat shops. Even backcourts aren't backcourts any more. In some versions of planner-speak they get called communal open space provision.

Although when tenements fell from favour the crash was thunderous, the nostalgia also remained heavy. Oh, dearie dear, the nostalgia. Much of it was mush. About warm memories of rows over the washing-house key, mistiest grew the eyes of former denizens who forgot how hard they'd fought their way out of the closes to purchase their nests in feudal Kilmacolm villas or Seamill bungalows. But there is so much remembered happiness as well. Lorna Hepburn, curator of the Tenement House in Buccleuch Street of the National Trust for Scotland, receives 20,000 visitors a year. She has seen refugees of tenement displacement break down in tears at the sight of her Zebo-gleaming kitchen range and even the five-bag coal bunker. 'We have kids who have never seen coal,' she said. 'Burning stones is a new idea to them.'

Social reconstruction of the idea of living up a close, though quick, has been hard to achieve. Equally not easy to explain is the old enthusiasm for it, even among those who dwell in the 12-room apartments of Hyndland or Dowanhill which are not so much just tenement houses as grand villas in the sky. Setting up house in an inhabited wall crowded with other families suggests a European fancy for courtyard living. It contrasts with the pride of the English that their home is their castle with a bit of garden for a moat. Anyhow, living on four shelves made sense in poor and chilly streets for how it kept down the cost of staying warm. Professor Andy MacMillan, professor of architecture at Glasgow University, a Maryhill boy and for long enough a lonely-voiced zealot for tenements, has piled into another explanation: 'Working-class men were too tired to work in gardens. They wanted to go out and drink some beer.'

On a sceptred isle of wasteland where Shakespeare Street meets Stratford Street in 1989 was completed a traditional tenement designed for modern living. Created by Maryhill Housing Association, its 56 houses are not truly Victorian only because to build in stone would have been too dear. But there are closes that are wally to the first floor. There are high-ceilinged front parlours. Behind the dark grey and buff concrete of the building there is a private backcourt.

Mother of the Stratford Street neighbourhood development is Jean McGuire, development chairman of the housing association, a lovely and formidable lady of ample heart and bosom, inexhaustible in her energy. High officials of the Scottish Office have been seen to quail before her. She used to be a bus conductress. Her new-old idea was so brilliantly simple she suffered sorely for it. One housing mandarin wanted to know if she had also a notion to bring back paraffin lamps. It took five battling years to get her tenement started. She said: 'I have always lived in a tenement. I was born in one. I can't see myself moving out of a tenement, except feet first. Even if you are unwell at home you can look out of the window and there is always something going on. If you live in a housing scheme, all you can see out of the house is somebody else's house.'

In an exploratory competition to fulfil their tenement dream the housing association had an international competition for architects with next-century ideas. Future visions arrived from faraway, exotic tenemental places, Edinburgh included, like Hong Kong and Zaire. One dotty design for living in Maryhill was crowned by a solar collector. And Jean McGuire was tickled by the whimsy of a plan that included a launching pad for Stratford Street's very own space shuttle.

*Troops turning into*
*Renfield Street from*
*Sauchiehall Street.*
*Probably 1915.*

*Let him who desires peace prepare for war: the 6th Battalion, the HLI, emerge at St Enoch Square on their way back from training at Gailes. Probably the late thirties.*

*The young John F. Kennedy (second from left) visited Glasgow in September 1939, and is seen here with some American survivors of the* Athenia *at the Central Hotel. The Lord Provost, Sir Patrick Dollan, is on Kennedy's right. The Glasgow-registered* Athenia, *with 1,400 passengers on board, sank after being torpedoed 200 miles west of the Hebrides.*

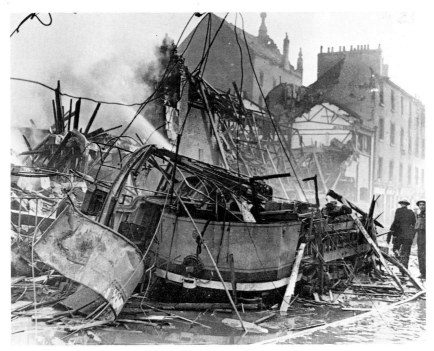

*Bombed tram in Nelson Street, 1940.*

Evacuation from Glasgow began in 1939. Because of the censor's restrictions, these children being evacuated from the Clyde by sea to South Africa in 1940 were said to be leaving from a 'British port'. In one picture the group's cheerfulness suggests they were enjoying the adventure: in the other a boy carries a disabled companion (a friend, perhaps, or a brother) on board.

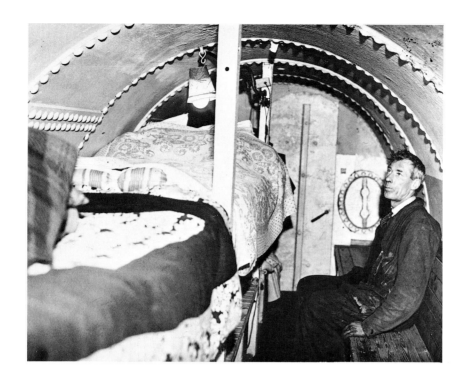

*Mr Robert Young invented a novel air-raid shelter by converting a ship's boiler which he erected on his front lawn; 1941.*

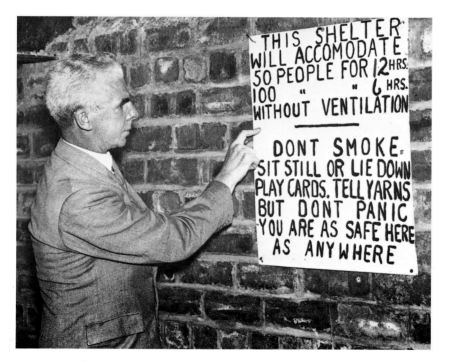

*Sir Patrick Dollan, Lord Provost from 1938 to 1941, studies the advice given, in a somewhat improvised notice, to people in an air-raid shelter. Those who bemoan current standards of literacy will note that certain words give trouble to all generations.*

*A bombed family carrying their possessions; undated but probably 1941.*

*Queuing for fuel
outside Tradeston Gas
Works, undated.*

*Evacuees at
Kelvinhaugh School
travelling from Kent
Road to Charing Cross
Station, probably 1941.*

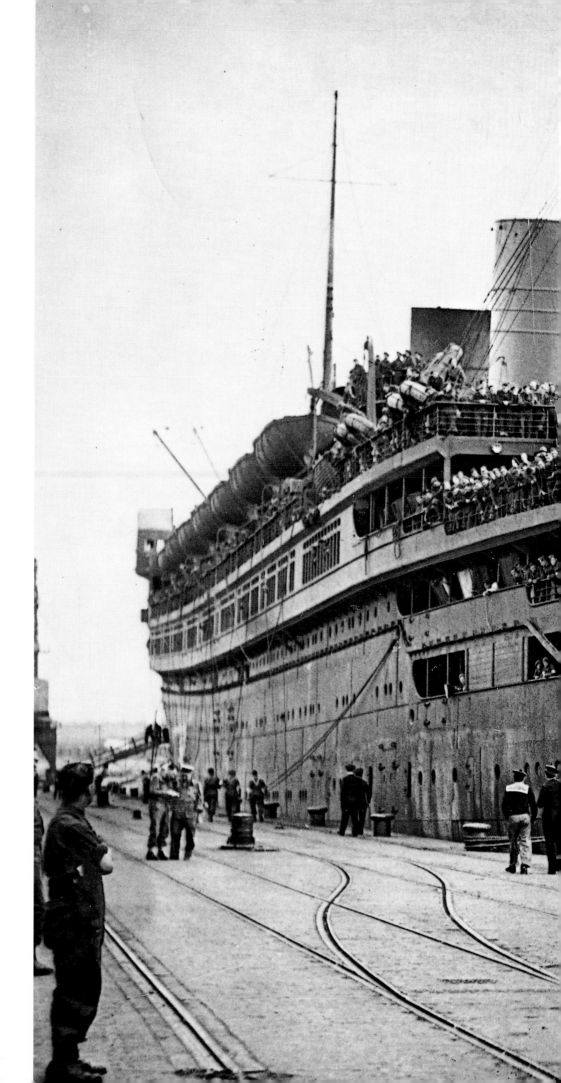

*Troopship on the Clyde. This picture is undated and marked 'Not passed by censor'. The ship is the* Monarch of Bermuda.

*Dad's Army. Home
Guard on parade, 1940.*

*Hail to the victor. Sir Winston Churchill on a tour of Glasgow on 28 June, 1945.*

*The ceremony in George Square on 9 June, 1945, to celebrate victory in Europe.*

*This is believed to be
the first news
photograph published
in the* Glasgow Herald,
*on 9 September, 1914.
It shows British
prisoners digging
trenches under the eye
of German guards.*

# Riverside Shuffle

Clyde, river, 106 miles long, many-watered. Daer, Elvan, Glengonner, Duneaton, Garf, Midloch and Medwyn have made it up; also the three Calders — North and South and Rotten — plus the Avon and the Mouse and both Carts, Black and White. Out from deepest Lanarkshire, Clyde came, shallowing uncertainly north, wondering which way to go . . . west-by-southward, south-westward, north-westward, so it passed Glasgow 'to the right' as the excellent Groome observes in his antique gazetteer.

Old Clyde came accidentally to the city. Confronted by a little lower obstacle at Biggar flatlands, it surely would have chosen to ooze more easily to the sea via Berwick. Instead, it went westwards and to work. Now it is the workingest river of all. Clyde creates electricity, costas holidays, cradles some ships, flushes the city of its filth . . . But its greatest creation is the city. Clyde made Glasgow and Glasgow made the Clyde. From time immemorial its waters have been mended, meaning made deeper, tirelessly dredged. Clyde — *clwyd*, strong — is man-made, less a river than a ditch. Yet, yes, its banks are sometimes bonnie.

*Glasgow Herald Review*, 1970

RUM HAS BEEN THE TREATMENT OF THE RIVER. AS WELL AS GOING UP AND down with the tide, the Clyde has kept going in and out from side to side. The song of the Clyde has been scored for a concertina. Before its banks were pushed in they were pulled out. And before that they had been pushed in. It is a canal of a river that has been allowed no peace on its bed.

Once upon a time the shallows at Broomielaw were, maybe, 300 feet across. Their water wandered through the mud to the sea. Engineers decided that wasn't business-like enough. They penned in the river by building dykes along it. That quickened the current. It also deepened the channel because the river started to scour its own bottom. Then a wide river was wanted back. More room was needed to berth boats. Holes for docks and basins were dug alongside the stream for extra parking. Next the holes got stuffed because they weren't wanted any more. Old man Clyde has never been allowed just to roll along. To catch the tides of industry the uses of the riverbanks have been shuffled from people to ships and back to people.

*Jamaica Bridge, 1896.*

People came first. Nature intended the Clyde for living beside. In earliest city days there were homes there, rather grand domiciles. It was where the merchants had their mansions. Plantation Quay took its name from the place of a moneybags who made his pile out of cotton. Building Kingston Dock was down to men who were given only shovels and

91

wheelbarrows for the job. Prince's Dock was the creation of one of the mightiest boats that ever was, a gravel-guzzling monster of a dredger called *Cairndhu*. With the docks away, the Clyde is back where it came in, with people. But they are land-livers in dolly brick tenements, the red ranch of a Post Office depot, another hotel, the cowsheds of the Scottish Exhibition Centre, with the remembered perfume of Garden Festival flowers. Is the Clyde chuckling that it might have been as well to leave it alone?

The obvious lazy way to get on with the building of ships and with import-export was at Greenock. Dragging harbour cargo by land to the Broomielaw would have needed less brilliant striving and hectic enterprise than the chosen way of water. As with the Clyde at Biggar, it was a narrow squeak that Glasgow took the turn it did. It's a thought that messing about with the width of the river could have been a mistake of big-headed ambition. It is a sweeter thought that in the new Jerusalem of little buildings along the waterfront there should be a bosky avenue called after the *Cairndhu*.

*The social privations endured by those on rent strike. This family's father, Walter Miller, was fighting for his country. The rent for the two-apartment house had been raised by 10d a month, making it £1 2s 10d.*

Many women took a leading role in the rent strikes, and most of the activists were members of the Independent Labour Party. The sign above the door casts the mind forward to contemporary protests about the poll tax.

*The part played by
women, and their
respectability, are
shown in this picture of
a social in Partick
Burgh Hall. The
protests led to an
industrial strike by
shipyard workers dnd
engineers and the
Government passed a
Rent Restriction Act
keeping rents at pre-
1914 levels, allowing an
increase only if repairs
were carried out.*

*The 1915 rent strike in Partick: a local newspaper editor, Mr Hood, addresses a crowd.*

*Strikes and unrest
continued after the First
World War. A strike at
Parkhead Forge led to
the imprisonment of
John Maclean, James
Maxton and others,
and this was the period
that earned the area the
nickname 'Red
Clydeside'. A campaign
for a 40-hour week led
to a strike in Glasgow
in 1919. Fears that this
might represent the
beginning of a Red
Revolution in Britain
(after the Bolshevik
Revolution in Russia
and revolutionary
upheavals in post-war
Germany) were
heightened by this
famous picture of the
Red Flag being raised in
George Square.*

*Emanuel Shinwell (left)
and Harry Hopkins
addressing the crowd in
George Square.*

*Civic dignitaries confer.
Sir James W. Stewart,
Lord Provost from
1917 to 1920, is third
from the left. Neil
McLean, the ILP MP
for Govan, is wearing
the soft hat.*

*John Maclean, the Marxist teacher, was a thorn in the Government's flesh during and after the war, paying for his beliefs with intermittent terms of imprisonment. Here he is shaking hands with the ILP's David Kirkwood during the 1919 strike. The ILP provided the 'Clydeside Brigade' — the ten Labour MPs (including Kirkwood) elected from Glasgow in the 1922 election. Maclean died in 1923.*

*Some of the strike leaders were arrested and tried at the High Court in Edinburgh. Left to right in the front row in the dock are: Emanuel Shinwell, Chairman of the strike committee and of Glasgow Trades Council; William Gallacher, shop stewards' leader; George Ebury, British Socialist Party; Harry Hopkins, District Secretary of the Engineers' Union; and James Murray. Shinwell was sentenced to five months' imprisonment, Gallacher and Murray to three; the others were found not guilty. The strike did not achieve a 40-hour week but hours were reduced for many workers after the war.*

*More than 700 witnesses were cited. This unusual picture shows the scene in the body of the court. Today it would be impossible to take, far less publish, such a picture without incurring the wrath of the bench.*

*Troops, seen preparing their evening meal in George Square, were called in.*

*The troops were stationed in the City Chambers and slept with weapons at hand.*

*During the General Strike of 1926 there were many conflicts between strikers and police, especially over the issue of 'blackleg' trains, buses and trams. Hundreds of arrests were made. Here an overturned bus is righted.*

*John McGovern, MP, addressing a 'free speech' meeting on Glasgow Green in 1931. Asked if he has a permit to address it, he replies that he does not intend asking for one.*

*The Depression years in the thirties produced the Hunger Marches. Harry McShane (in bonnet) and John McGovern (right), Labour MP for Shettleston from 1920 to 1959, lead a protest march to Edinburgh in 1933. McGovern died in 1968 and McShane in 1988 at the grand old age of 96.*

*A soup kitchen in Airdrie, 1933. Sir James Knox serves the unemployed. The scheme was self-supporting and a charge of a penny was made for a bowl of soup and a piece of bread.*

*A small group of the women's section of the Community Service for Unemployment Central Club in West Nile Street, 1938.*

*The great Lloyd George made many visits to Glasgow. In 1915, at the height of working-class militancy, a meeting designed to mobilise the war effort addressed by him in the St Andrew's Hall ended in disorder. The newspaper* Forward *was subsequently suppressed because of its uninhibited account of events. Here, in 1935, he is seen addressing a meeting in the same place with the same theme — the mobilisation of national resources. The platform party on this calmer occasion includes Sir Andrew Pettigrew (extreme left), the Marchioness of Aberdeen beside Sir D. M. Stevenson and Sir Robert Horne (extreme right).*

*The First World War radicalised Glasgow politics. The engineering and shipbuilding industries attracted thousands to work in war production but appalling housing conditions became worse as landlords raised rents and evicted tenants who did not pay. By October 1915 some 25,000 tenants were on rent strike.*

# Bright Lights

—Ur ye dancin'?
—Ur ye askin'?
—Ah'm askin'.
—Ah'm dancin'.
Formal dancehall dialogue

WHEN ON A WET NIGHT IN MAY THE ALHAMBRA THEATRE SHUT, ON THE BILL was George Chisholm, maestro of the trombone, comic — and cinema accompanist. His first job was at Dalmarnock pictures, a swanky hall that in 1921 had earned a paragraph in the *Herald* when it became a £25,000 dream-palace addition to cinema city. Young Chisholm played a piano to muscle the action of Ramon Navarro and the likes of *Ben-Hur*. He provided music for newsreels. His father, also George Chisholm, was a drummer but not an ordinary one. He was The Original Singing Drummer. With his right hand he tapped a drumstick, while in the left he held a megaphone to croon through. The family lived in what used to be South Portland Street. 'Nostalgia for me is mainly going about to see places that aren't there any more,' George Chisholm says when he comes back.

Not there nowadays is the Tower Ballroom, one of the dancingest arenas in town, up a close in Possil. He recalled: 'There were these guys who used to march about the floor keeping the best of order and shouting (he put on his radio *Goon Show* voice): "Nae burlin'".' The big-time was Green's Playhouse ballroom, nine floors up on top of the picture house. He said: 'Off the floor and up a stair there was this kind of lavatory. That was the band room. One night there was a knock at the little window. It was a fan we had — Big Adam. "Here ah am, boys," he cried. He had climbed up the rone because he was barred. They were always throwing him out. So they grabbed him and threw him out again.'

On the night the Alhambra died Chis was the only home-produced talent on the show. Cilla Black was top. There was a north of England drunk, a Continental bicycle team, and a kind of barber's shop quartet (actually six of them, with a drum which changed colour). Whoever killed vaudeville, that night in 1969 vaudeville struck back. The Alhambra, aged 58, the premier theatre, abune them all for dressy spectaculars, complex multi-directional stage machinery, a sunken swimming pool and imported artists with stardust on their names, went out pure music hall. Herbert Lumsden, the manager, wept. The programme sellers wept. In the thronged bars there were tears. But there was champagne. Bert Lumsden's house was spruce and groomed and efficient as always. There were some good jokes, albeit only from the audience. 'Tell Charlie,' one paying mourner at the wake shouted to his neighbour two seats away about *his* neighbour a further two off, 'tell Charlie to speak up. Half the audience can't hear him,' he bellowed. Meanwhile, in the show, an English droll was suffering. He hooted: 'Ooh, the wife. She's a redhead. No hair. Just a red head.' It seemed that the Alhambra had been sentenced to die like an elephant — slowly, a bit at a time, utterly. Then there was Cilla.

She appeared in a plain luxuriantly coloured gown on a bare gorgeously lit stage. She sang a little. She sounded off in that Scouse voice. She chucked insults. She provoked. She sang a little again. She had them clapping. She insulted some more. She fought them all the way. Suddenly, she had wrapped the packed audience around her as if they were only a few boys and girls in the backroom. What would they have? 'We'll try "Bye Bye Blackbird",' she said down into the pit. She busked straight in. Unbriefed, the musicians of the Alhambra's precision orchestra busked after her gamely. Then 'Always' (I'll be loving you ALWAYS); 'You Made Me Love You', 'I didn't want to do it. I didn't want to do it,' they roared in her wake.

All demure and subdued, Cilla deemed it a great honour to lead them into 'Auld Lang Syne'. As everybody stood up there was the ragged machine-gun fire of the tipping back of seats. Spasmodic artillery answered as the attendants clanked open the exits. Cold damp blasts swept in from the real world. Two quick curtains. The end. Into where the Alhambra was has been put a filing cabinet of a government office, glum as any other government office.

*Underground scene in the fifties. Some people have a nostalgia for the vanished smell of the old Subway, a smell described by some as of rotting straw.*

*Sailing down the Clyde:
the band plays on for
the holiday crowd as
the* King Edward *leaves
the Broomielaw, July
1939.*

*Holidaymakers crowd the platform at Central Station on the first day of the Fair in July 1942.*

*The first Fair after the war. Crowds gather early in the morning at Buchanan Street station at the end of June, 1946.*

*Classic Fair family
party, 1951. Note that
the pram is not used for
carrying the wean.*

*The young ladies of Laurelbank School wave farewell as they set off on what was probably the biggest adventure of their young lives — a trip to France for Easter, April 1955.*

*D9 (39)*
*Huntly & Palmers Biscuits, Ovaltine, steam trains and National Service. Queen Street Station, June 1954.*

*Eager holidaymakers
hurry to secure seats on
the Saltcoats and Largs
train. Easter Monday at
St Enoch Station, April
1955.*

119

*Goodbye to the trams,*
*September 1962.*
*Somebody somewhere*
*must have that penny as*
*a souvenir of the*
*parade.*

*The interior of a streamlined tram, undated.*

*The Glasgow Underground in 1968 before its renovation. Conductor Charlie Johnston with driver Davie Allen (right).*

*The Underground
platform at St Enoch,
1955.*

*Grave news in the
comic today, my dear.
Young holidaymakers,
July 1941.*

*Central Station in 1937.*

*A photographer or picture librarian of the day added the caption to this picture from 1936: 'A form of transport now, unfortunately, obsolete.'*

# Red to Orange

Oh, it's lovely going your holidays.
On the Glasgow Underground.
*The Glasgow Underground,* by CLIFF HANLEY

WHILE THE TRAMS RETAIN THE GLORY, THE SUBWAY HAS KEPT GOING. IT WINS minds more than hearts. Keelie travellers remain uneasy about having to sit and stare at each other. Maybe the Subway is too efficient to be funny, although in its toytown way it's that as well. Give it long enough, it never goes anywhere except right back where it started from. But it is a roundabout that has magic which attracts an unspoken, deep affection of the lieges. To declare a proprietorial interest, it was a headline in the *Herald* that gave the name of Clockwork Oranges to the second fleet of trains. In the beginning the carriages were red. They were hauled by cables. Mothers used to take sick children down below in the belief that station smells of tarry ropes could cure the whooping cough.

The Subway story has circulated for a century. Back in 1891 a way was sought through an unknown underworld from a hole in the ground at St Enoch. Ten times a reluctant tunnel blew out under the Clyde. Between Govan Cross and Merkland Street two tunnellers died in a fire. Total cost to the Subway company was £1.1 million. After Glasgow Corporation had taken over, they electrified the traction in 1935. It was then that officially — but only officially — the Subway became the Underground.

Until the ramshackle wooden trains tottered to their death they never saw daylight, until they were knackered in 1977. The survival for so long of their Victorian timber was a kind of biological miracle. Even the Subway craftsmen at the Govan sheds were in some awe of their own achievement. About how they had held the carriages in one piece all they said was that they had kept using longer nails.

When the system was rebuilt it became the hole with two mints of money in it. Around £35 million was the reckoning for the Clockwork Oranges. Sundry items of modernisation included lifting the dwarf's castle of the information shop at St Enoch station by eight millimetres because its foundations were found to be resting on the roof of the tunnel. A corner of the former home of the Royal College of Music and Drama was discovered to be resting on three feet of nothing much at all. Despite all the improvements, the idea was to keep the Subway experience much the same, which is to say huddled and cosy — except they took the shoogle out along with the remembered, ancient smell.

When the first new coach made its maiden run it travelled for 50 smooth yards there and back in a straight line above ground at the Govan sheds. 'It still has the intimacy of the old system,' Tom Fulton, chairman of Strathclyde's Highways and Transportation Committee, said. The *Herald* Diary said: 'Glasgow will find its own name for the stylish new carriages. For going on with, however, permit them to be called here the Clockwork Oranges.'

*Castlebank Street, Partick, undated.*

*The tram and the horse and cart are familiar Glasgow street themes down the years. Jamaica Street looking north towards Argyle Street, 1905.*

*Dumbarton Road near*
*Partick Cross, undated.*

*The tramway shelter,*
*Battlefield, 1915.*

*A Glasgow funeral, Mr 'Fivers' Watson is buried in the Gallowgate. He achieved local fame as a horse dealer. From the turnout at his funeral one may guess that he was an honest man, undated.*

*The tea-room and the coffee-house were important institutions. Wendy's tea-room, 1933.*

*Christmas shopping in the Argyll Arcade, 1934.*

*Cooper's Tea Room,
Ingram Street, in the
fifties. Charles Rennie
Mackintosh was the
interior architect.*

*Trams and trolleybuses
in the snow, 1947.*

*Alexandra Parade,*
*1947.*

*Lums, middens and distant roofs: a smoky townscape from 1947. The camera is looking towards Montrose Street and Parliamentary Road from the roof of the maternity hospital in Rotten Row.*

*Apple-seller Lizzie Dale,*
*1949.*

*Chestnut-vendor, 1949.*

*Again the horse, cart and trams. Union Street in November, 1948.*

139

*Springburn in the fifties.*
*The importance of the*
*Co-op is evident: the*
*age of the supermarket*
*has not yet dawned.*

*The fruit market in*
*Candleriggs, 1955. It*
*has since moved — for*
*reasons of congestion*
*which this picture*
*makes evident.*

140

*The old Adelphi Hotel,*
*much used by the SFA,*
*1957.*

*An early view of the
Barras, undated.*

*Street vendor at the
Barras, 1949.*

*Busker in Buchanan
Street, 1955.*

*Martin Breedis, 70,*
*balances a 220lb weight*
*on his foot, 1954.*

*The Barras in 1955.*

*Stow Street at its
meeting with
Cowcaddens Street,
looking towards
Queen's Arcade, 1956.*

*The art of the salesman:
the Barras in 1956.*

*Queen's Arcade, 1956.*

*Flower-seller in Union
Street, 1956.*

*The steamie made wash-day sociable. It has since been celebrated as an institution in the popular play of the same name by Tony Roper. The universal usefulness of the pram is also illustrated in this picture of the Kingston washhouse from 1957.*

*Kingston washhouse, 1957.*

*The coin-in-the-slot*
*ironing machine.*
*Kingston washhouse,*
*1957.*

*Kingston washhouse,*
*1957.*

*Herbert Byatt with his*
*one-string fiddle, 1957.*

*Two buskers trawl the
queue at the Odeon,
1959.*

*Gorbals funeral of an eight-year-old girl killed by a lorry near her home. Her father, beginning a sentence for housebreaking and safeblowing, was allowed out of Barlinnie for the day.*

*Dorothy Parker said that nobody has any business going around looking like a horse. For some, in the fruit market in 1964, the comparison was unavoidable.*

*Contemplation amid
the cabbages. Fruit
market, 1964.*

*Last days of the leeries.*
*A lamplighter in*
*Gorbals in the sixties.*

160

*The National Trust for Scotland's Tenement House in Buccleuch Street, 1987.*

*Gorbals street scene,*
*1964.*

*Tableau vivant with car.*
*The view from*
*Roystonhill towards the*
*Red Road flats, 1969.*

*Scene in a tenement,*
*1970.*

*The kitchen range was an indispensable part of tenement life. It heated the home and cooked the food, producing particularly delicious stews. But it was a domestic tyrant because it had to be black-leaded. This picture from 1977 shows it in its last days.*

*Craig's Restaurant on the day of its closure in 1955.*

166

# At War

I once spoke to a young soldier who was born and bred in genuinely metropolitan London. He had begun his army career in Bournemouth and then had been transferred to Glasgow. When I suggested that he must have regretted the change, he looked at me as if I had suddenly been bereft of my senses, if any. Bournemouth he regarded as a kind of semi-final for the cemetery, but Glasgow was alive, pulsing with bonhomie and uninhibited enjoyment of this, that and the other. He had had the best time of his life in Glasgow, and the London that he knew was a flat and friendless place in comparison.

*The Glasgow Story*, by COLM BROGAN

GEORGE SQUARE, AUGUST WITH COUNCILLORS AND STOOKIES, HAD A RAKISH past. It was a Bohemian enclave. For café society, formal feasting and hotel life it was the very place. Gossip was a lively part of its business. It was where to go for the tittle-tattle of the town. Briefly, during the Hitler war, it was the main source of the world's rumour mill when the old walls of the square's North British Hotel were the first to hear whispers of one of the handful of big secrets of this century.

At a small dinner party were Lord Provost Paddy Dollan and Tom Johnston, from Kirkintilloch, mightiest of Secretaries of State for Scotland. A few local dignitaries attended. Also present was Winston Churchill, the Prime Minister. With them was a frail American who looked white-faced and unwell. He was Harry Hopkins, a personal envoy of President Franklin D. Roosevelt, who was returning from Scapa Flow to London with Churchill. It was a social nosh, with wives there.

In his efforts to swing US opinion towards the war, Roosevelt had sent Harry Hopkins to see what a fist Britain was making of the fight. Whatever signals he was sending back nobody knew, not even Churchill. There wasn't a hint from Harry Hopkins. 'Dumb as an oyster,' Tom Johnston wrote in his *Memories* (1952). After the dinner he had a clever little notion — he insisted it was only an impulse — to ask Mr Hopkins if he'd like to say a word. For a few sentences the man from Washington nattered about this and that. Tom Johnston regretted afterwards that he could never remember about what. Quietly, Harry Hopkins drifted into mentioning that his grannie had come from Auchterarder, Perthshire, and how well she had read her Bible.

He looked straight down the table at Churchill to add: 'Wheresoever thou goest we go, and where thou lodgest we lodge, thy people shall be our people, thy God, our God, even unto the end.'

He sat down. There was silence around the table. Churchill's eyes filled with tears. The Yanks were coming.

*ARP (Air Raid Precautions) women clear the streets after a snowfall in February 1942.*

*Mrs Janet Chisholm tends the Eastwood signalbox, 1942.*

*At work in Springburn Women's Training Centre, 1941.*

*Women lamplighters,
undated.*

*Working on the
railways, probably
1942.*

Washing seats at
Hampden Park, 1939.

Elizabeth Davidson of
Parkhead, one of the
first women guards on
the LNER, in action at
Queen Street Station,
1943.

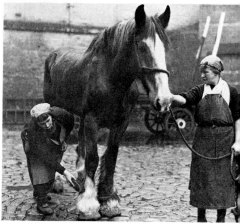

*Women at work in the LMS stables in Glasgow, 1941.*

*A thoroughly modern mum. Four-year-old Gerald Blythe congratulates his mother Isabel after her graduation with an MA honours in social sciences, 1984.*

*Interior of a curtain
factory, Glasgow, 1919.*

# Some Revolting
# Gentlemen

I am not here as the accused: I am here as the accuser of capitalism
dripping with blood from head to foot.
JOHN MACLEAN at his trial for sedition

IN THE HERALD'S MOST FAMOUS LIBRARY PICTURE EVERYBODY HAS A HAT ON.
Most of them not in police helmets wear bunnits, sometimes called
doolanders, meaning caps constructed of so much cloth that a pigeon
could have used them for a runway. There are several bowler hats because
keeping under cover was only sensible. When strikers for a 40-hour week
battled with the constabulary in George Square in 1919 it was the last day
of January. Yet it is strange now to see all of them, or nearly, so formal.
Their bunnits look like best, or Sunday, ones. The crowd are dressed for a
parade and not a punch-up. These were not ragged-trousered revolutionaries. Nor were most of the early leaders of the industrial working
class. If one word suits the agitators whose names have become embalmed
in proletarian memory, it is perjink.

Maclean favoured a Homburg. Shinwell and Kirkwood were dressy. If
Maxton looked as if he had fallen off somebody else's clothes-peg,
Gallacher, Neil McLean and Wheatley were turned out nice. Harry
McShane, last of the Red Clydesiders, was a most dapper rebel. His
morning shave was surgical. Collar and tie appeared to have been
moulded to his neck. He explained: 'I am an engineer. Engineers always
used to put on their blue suits and their bowler hats to the Kirk on
Sundays.' As well as being tradesmen they were gentlemen. In every
remaining good sense of the word they were toffs. They liked a laugh and,
with the serious exception of John Maclean, they made jokes: in their
Edinburgh prison Willie Gallacher said goodnight to Jimmy Maxton by
tapping out the Red Flag on the wall.

Glasgow remembers them not just as scholars, orators, street generals,
and pamphleteers, but decent men. Opponents (and individual policemen)
respected them, while detesting their politics. Although the best of them
never surrendered, it has helped to mellow their group memory that
some of them enjoyed great age. Gallacher attained 73 years and (Lord)
Kirkwood 82. When Harry McShane was 86 he said: 'It occurred to me
this morning when I was getting up that in another few years, if I live, I'll
be 90, and then I'll be old.' He reached 96 and (Lord) Shinwell was 101
when he died.

Saintly John Maclean (44), daddy of them all, the most revered, remains
the enigma. When artist Ken Currie was creating a charcoal drawing for
the People's Palace he said: 'In every picture I've found of him he looks
different.' In the Russian postage stamp which commemorates Daddy

Maclean he might be a boxing trainer. His photos make him out to be several men from the Pru. He was a Glasgow rabble-rouser who never drank. He didn't smoke. Towards the end he did not eat a lot either. A pauper's diet of dates and pease-brose kept him going for a time. Before he caught fatal pneumonia he had given away his overcoat to a poorer man. Maybe, just mebbe, he had one ordinary human weakness. Recent research suggests that on some Saturday afternoons he slipped out of the real and brutish world. From his empty terrace house in Newlands he'd put his hat on his head and go over the hill to Hampden when Queen's Park were at home. He went alone to give a shout for the Spiders. There's perjink.

*The Clarkston Disaster of 1952: the search for survivors.*

*Cheapside Street fire:*
*the reckoning, 1960.*

*Disgraceful scenes at the Hampden cup final between Celtic and Rangers in 1980 were among the incidents that led to the decision to ban drink at football grounds. WPC Elaine Mudie (now Simpson) and her white horse Ballantrae were in the thick of things. In 1989 Ballantrae retired from police work to a school for disabled riders. Celtic won 1-0.*

*The loss by fire in 1962 of St Andrew's Hall, the acoustics of which were prized by musicians, left a gap in Glasgow's musical life that has persisted until 1990 and the new concert hall.*

*Sixty-six fans were killed in the Ibrox disaster of 4 January, 1971. Fans leaving early turned back when they heard the roar for a late goal, and the stanchions collapsed on Stair 13. The score that day was Rangers 1, Celtic 1.*

*Fire in Argyle Street, 1949. Watched by milling crowds, a woman is rescued by firemen.*

*Nineteen firemen and Salvage Corps personnel died at a whisky bond in Cheapside Street in 1960. The side of the warehouse building collapsed on to the men and a parked fire engine. In the foreground is a lamp set up by firemen.*

# Coffee Stop

The atmosphere of this place, confounded mist from the Highlands and
smoke from the factories, is crushing my eyebrows as I write, and it rains
as it never does rain anywhere else, and always does it rain here. It is a
dreadful place . . .
CHARLES DICKENS

YES, IT IS SOMETIMES WET AND THERE USED TO BE FOGS WHICH WERE FOUL.
Less observant visitors than Charlie Dickens have noticed. People from
Manchester have noticed. Sometimes the natives have thought the rain
worth a remark. They used to like to concede there were days that even
Gene Kelly wouldn't go out in. And several postcards home by travellers
have been less than jolly. Dorothy Wordsworth tut-tutted: 'I also could
not but observe a want of cleanliness in the appearance of the lower
orders of the people.' Poets have found their muse running cold. To Hugh
MacDiarmid the keelies were cowardly, untrustworthy, and lascivious. 'A
gutted city inhabited by gnomes,' opined J. F. Hendry. Another chiel who
took notes about how oppressed he felt by the weather was H. V. Morton.
He can come again, though. The few complaints he made are redeemed by
one shining sentence. In *In Search of Scotland* (1929) he wrote: 'To know
a man by sight is to ask him to have a coffee at 11 a.m.' In high style he
went on to insist that, if the Clyde ever ran dry, enough coffee was
consumed every morning to float the biggest Cunarder.

Glaswegians have always loved their own street life. Whatever the
weather, they went out in it. A wee refreshment helped. Although always
at least plentifully pubbed, their oasis pleasures were best taken in smoke-
filled coffee-shops and ornately douce tea-rooms. They were places of
business as well. Hugh Fraser (Lord Fraser of Allander) switched his shop
group's bank account to another bank after he happened to sit next to a
branch manager he took a shine to at a morning coffee. When he joined
the family business from school his first innovation was to enlarge the tea-
room. Ladies had havens of their own from away back in 1888 when the
Colosseum store opened an exclusive salon for stylish *café au lait* and
Continental pastries.

It was jumping on and off the trams for a ha'penny fare that gave the
streets of the old city their bustle and pace. But it was (in an H. V. Morton
phrase) its Tokyo of tea-houses and its dark-brown coffee shops which
nurtured the wary chumminess and warmth of commercial life, and not
just at 11 a.m. The same cronies deserted their office stools to meet again
in the afternoon. It fair put the hems on the bevvying.

181

*Launch of the* Queen Elizabeth: *workmen take five on the huge drag chains being readied for the launch, 1938.*

*Opening of King George V Dock, 1931.*

*A bustling scene of commerce, 1932. The Dalriada is berthed beside King George V Bridge. In the background, on the other side of the Clyde, is the clock-tower of John Knox Church.*

*Clydeside workers enjoying their dinner break, 1959.*

*Launch of the* Queen
Mary, *1934.*

*The* Queen Mary
*leaving the Clyde, 1934.*

*The* Queen Elizabeth *in
the fitting-out basin,
1938.*

*Fishing vessels at
Custom House Quay,
1943.*

*The* Patonga *launched
from Stephen's yard.
Anchored alongside is
the Greek ship*
Olympia, *1953.*

187

*The* QEII: *the great ship enters the water.*

*There is always something magical about the launch of a great ship. The Queen and Princess Margaret set the* Queen Elizabeth II *on her way, 1968.*

# Photo Finish

Photie: short for photograph, but sometimes applied to any picture: 'She's awful holy; she's got the hoose full a saints' photies.'
*The Patter,* by MICHAEL MUNRO

DESPITE ITS FAME, ONE PHOTOGRAPH HAS NO RIGHT TO BE INCLUDED. IT IS AN illicit snap. History should not be able to see into the dock at the trial of some of the strike leaders of the 1919 battle of George Square. As now, photography in court was taboo. At last it can be revealed how the deed was done. A photographer whose name has been forgotten conjured the picture out of his bowler hat, a badge of the early photo-snatchers. Once upon a time judges were relaxed about turning a blind eye when picture journalists sat on the press benches with their bowlers on their laps. Behind their hard hats were hidden small plate cameras, sometimes called detective cameras. When the bowler was put aside, a controlled cough covered the short, near-silent click of the shutter.

In the three-quarters of a century since the *Herald* first printed news pictures there have been only three chief photographers, each a legend. The late David L. Stewart, who had sharpened his technique in the Royal Flying Corps, was the first staff cameraman. The immortal action study of Alan Morton of Rangers and Scotland is one of his. Dunky Stewart was a favourite photographer of the Queen Mother who took one of his prints for her Christmas cards.

Henry McKenzie Robertson Bain Moyes, usually called Mister Moyes, was the next headman until he retired in 1974. Inside his trade, Harry Moyes became the best-known newspaperman in Scotland and the best-loved — taproom philosopher, wayward servant, patient teacher, bonnie mate, gentle man. A dab hand in a darkroom, he takes marvellous pictures because he loves people, and it shows. His feet are the funniest since Chaplin. He never knows the time. In this book John Mackay, the *Herald's* chief photographer, is also one of a kind for how he stars on both sides of the camera. When he was felled by a flying cabbage at the Rab Butler rectorial rammie, his colleagues demonstrated the instant warm camaraderie of their professionalism. Some of them smartly propped up his fallen body to get a clearer shot of him.

If all newspaper photographers share one characteristic it has something to do with a knack for disciplined desperation and a gift for prowling, alert patience. If they have a common addiction it lies in an urge to consume their own weight in film every day. A product of their constant clicking lies in the treasure of 5½ million prints in the Outram Picture Library, housed between the editorial floors of the *Herald* and the *Evening Times*. About 300, sometimes 400, pictures are added from around the world every day. The four filing librarians are also the guardians of an historic collection of Scottish pictures, the Outram archive's photographic memory of everyday living in Scotland.

Most of the early pictures were taken or collected for the *Bulletin* newspaper, a pictorial daily of lamented memory. Because the *Bulletin* began in 1915, the Outram Picture Library probably started about the same time. But that's a guess. It is a library which just started to grow. Bill Doig, the picture librarian, says: 'It is likely that one day somebody just decided that some of the stuff he was handling should be kept.'

The library's clients include foreign magazines, television documentaries, university presses and even national art galleries. Outram pictures have illustrated learned volumes about shipbuilding and engineering, while homelier snaps have helped to brighten earnest books of local history. But this is the first time the library that just grew has had a book to itself. About half the work of the photographers has not seen the light of day before, not even in the old *Bulletin*.

*Jamaica Bridge, 1896.*

# Appendix

PICTURE EDITORS
J. McLatchie *deceased*, Alex Burnie *deceased*, G. Keith Blount, Douglas Bottomley, George Wilkie, Alistair Stars.

PICTURE DESK
James Blake *deceased,* George Lawrie *deceased,* Jack Scrimgeour, Gordon Rule, Tom Fitzpatrick, Ian Elder, Bill Law, Nigel Hill, James Connor.

PHOTOGRAPHERS
H. Cook *deceased,* George Simpson *deceased,* Chris Macrae *deceased,* D. L. Stewart MBE *deceased,* H. M. Moyes, James Thompson, John Mackay, James Millar, Stuart Paterson, Duncan Dingsdale, Edward Jones, Arthur Kinloch, Ian Hossack, James Galloway, Angela Catlin, James Hamilton, Robin Gray, Craig Halkett, James Mackey, John Young, Bill Fleming, Bert Paterson, Alastair Devine.

INFORMATION MANAGER
David Ball.

PICTURE LIBRARY
Bill Doig (picture librarian), Robert Tweedie, Jim McNeish, Malcolm Beaton, Tony Murray, Grace Wilson, Wilma Barrows.

PHOTO PRINTERS
Ronald Gordon, Hugh McLean, Ronald McKechnie, Ronald Scott, Bill Love, Gilbert Stronach, George McAloon, Ian Pratt.

EDITORIAL LIBRARY
Marie Jordan (head librarian), Chris Boyce, Marie Campbell, Annie Cunningham, Catherine Turner, Stroma Fraser, Maris Macfarlane, Kathleen Smith, Beverley Mercer, Jane Challinor.

CAPTIONS RESEARCHER
John Hutcheson.